How to Access Jesus in the Heavenly Realm

A Manual by
Kim Robinson

Book design / Dorothea LeBlanc

www. Heavenisfun.com

brightlights-kim@att.net

Printed in the United States of America.

INTRODUCTION

Since 1988 the Holy Spirit has been taking me to Heaven. Jesus would show me various fun places and allow me to do fun things. I asked, "Why was He showing me these places?" Jesus said, "Because people think all they do here is float around wearing diapers, eating grapes, or doing nothing but bowing before Me. I have planned for each person, in detail, what makes them happy to be here with Me. So, you are to tell them Heaven is real and FUN, and Jesus is coming soon!"

Jerry and Kim Robinson have five children, and ten grandchildren with more on the way. Kim is the liaison at Joppa House of Prayer in Bentonville, AR. for a Sozo Ministry; healing hearts is her passion. Kim is a part of the prayer team at a local church in Bentonville where she and her husband, Jerry Robinson have attended, for over 10 years. Jerry is retired, loves golf and is an amazing cook.

Kim has written "HEAVEN is real and FUN" which is also in audio form available from her website. She has also written "Jesus is real and FUN" a children's activity book. They may be purchased from her website www.heavenisfun.com.

CONTACT

Contact Kim at brightlights-kim@att.net or
at her "Heaven is real and FUN" Facebook page.
Also, please check out her YouTube channel, "Heaven is real and FUN"
for more teachings. For more information please go to:
www.heavenisfun.com

TABLE OF CONTENTS

ENDORSEMENTS

"In the Bible, it is written that we are seated with Jesus in heavenly places. Throughout the Bible, it talks about our spirit being called up to the Heavens by Our Father. When I heard about Kim Robinson and read her adventures with Jesus, in her book 'Heaven Is Real And Fun,' I knew that Heavenly encounters were truly possible. In her latest book 'How to Access Jesus in the Heavenly Realm - Manual: Heaven is Real and FUN,' Kim helps you to walk step by step with Jesus exploring this unseen realm. I love how Kim uses the beautiful simplicity of coming to Jesus as a little child. This is going to help open your eyes to a whole new world wrapped up in The Father's love."

Lisa Perna

"I am honored to endorse such an amazing manual. In this manual, you will find practical steps to help you get into the presence of God. Kim gives you key access points (Jesus, the scriptures) that will help you in your journey to know Him better. I love the fact that she also addresses hindrances and roadblocks so that you can quickly move any obstacle out of the way. Kim is sharing her revelation so you too can access the Heavenly realm, as you were created to do. Kim also gives practical steps to position yourself (for the more logical thinkers) to experience the fullness of being a son or daughter of the most high. I can feel the Holy Spirit's heart on this book as I read it – and you will too. Bravo Kim!

April Stutzman Co-founder, Kingdom Flame Ministries
www.kingdomflameministries.com

"What a beautiful treasure Kim Robinson is to the Body of Christ and those who are coming into the Kingdom for such a time as this. This manual is an amazing key for those whose hearts burn with the desire to engage with Yeshua. The only requirement we have to engage with our home (Heaven) and our Bridegroom lover, is childlike faith! Kim is teaching people to have childlike faith to enter into a portion of their inheritance as believers.

Kim is one of many who have been going in and out of Heaven, and her testimony is verified by more than 3 witnesses. I highly recommend this training manual to anyone who is hungry for more of Yeshua, more of Papa God, more of HolySpirit and more of the things of heaven.

This manual is the incredible companion to take you into your own experiences with Yeshua. Heaven is our home and the more we know, the more we can take the sting out of death for those who are lost. Now is the time to preach the Kingdom on earth as it is in Heaven. You can't do that if you don't know what Heaven is like!

I also recommend getting Kim's first book called, 'Heaven is Real and Fun' so you can learn about and imagine all the places in Heaven that she describes. The imagination is our built-in connection to the spirit realm, it is where faith works to produce substance. Heaven is real and it is totally fun! Go for it and enjoy every minute. "

Bernadette Joy Elder (Apostle B.Joy)
Love Warriors... Love Feasts to Start a Love Revolution

ACKNOWLEDGEMENTS

I would like to express my gratitude and thank the following for all they have done:

Dorothea C. M. LeBlanc for her help in the editing and layout of this book.

My husband *Jerry* for letting me take the time to write and for keeping hot food on the table.

My friends *Shuntu* and *Vonda* for the miles we walked together while talking about doing this manual, and for their encouragement.

STATEMENT

In this manual I will walk you through how you may access the presence of Jesus in the heavenly realm by the Holy Spirit.

When the Holy Spirit first took me to Jesus I didn't know how to do this, but I will try to articulate what I have learned.

The bottom line is, 'Just TRUST the Holy Spirit.'

Find intimate time to spend with Jesus. Trust Jesus, and let Him take you to the Father. It really is that easy!

Children are seeing Jesus, Angels, and the Father— and you can too!

Kim Robinson

However, as it is written: "What no eye has seen, what no ear has heard, and what no human mind has conceived" those things God has prepared for those who love him — these are the things God has revealed to us by his Spirit. The Spirit searches all things, even the deep things of God. (1 Corinthians 2: 9-10)

And many peoples shall go and say, Come ye, and let us go up to the mountain of Jehovah, to the house of the God of Jacob; and he will teach us of his ways, and we will walk in his paths: for out of Zion shall go forth the law, and the word of Jehovah from Jerusalem. (Isaiah 2:3 ASV)

SESSION ONE: OPENING

I receive questions almost daily about how to access Jesus and Heaven. It occurred to me that there is a real interest in people's hearts to know this, so I have decided to put in writing what I find myself retelling.

This isn't a formula but just a starting place to maybe help guide you, or to confirm what the Holy Spirit has already been saying to you.

It is very simple but you first have to make the time to spend with Jesus. Plan the time and place to get quiet and to be alone with Jesus.

Do we treat Jesus like the old elderly family dog? Saying, "Hi" when we first wake up in the morning, but ignore him the rest of the day except for maybe a passing pat on the head or a stroke of the hair. Then late at night before we go to bed, do we scratch the dog under the chin telling them, "How much we love them and what a great dog they are?"

Let's spend more quality time with Jesus than we do with the elderly pets that we so dearly love and cherish.

It may seem to you that early in the morning before work is a good time for short encounters with Jesus. Some people find that in the evening they have more time to go to a prayer room or other location for their alone, intimate time with Jesus, the Father, and the Holy Spirit.

Once you have entered this time that you have set aside, you may want to put on some praise music. Spend some time singing out loud to Jesus, the Father, and the Holy Spirit.

This time of praise brings your body and soul into alignment with God's heart.

You may have to train your soul, or your mind to stay focused on Jesus, and not wander through the daily tasks you had or may have ahead of you.

Sing in your prayer language (tongues), or your own language, out loud. Sing a new song to Jesus, and don't worry if it isn't in tune or rhymes. Begin to enjoy Jesus' presence and the freedom you will feel.

Don't rush or hurry through this intimate time. Remember Jesus has been waiting to spend this time with you. He wants to talk and share His heart with you. Spend this time with Jesus because you want to be with Him, not because you want to receive revelation (so you can have a ministry).

How would it make you feel if you had a friend who wanted to be your friend and spend time with you just because you had a ministry or just because they wanted to be a part of your ministry? Kind of used?

Don't use this intimate time with Jesus as a ministry tool, but relax and enjoy your time with Him. Just chill!

Talk to Jesus, the Father, and the Holy Spirit. After a while, you will begin to feel the shift in your heart to go to a more intimate level.

Continue praying in tongues – or you may read scriptures – or both, reading the scriptures and focusing on one verse. Ask Jesus to speak to you about this one verse. Or ask, Jesus to take you to "this scripture location" in time. That is also an incredible experience. The scriptures are portals, which means the scriptures are doorways; gates or entrances into God's heart or thoughts.

To help your thoughts or mind not be so engaged, you might prefer to read scriptures first.

You may now want to put on some worship music or what I call soaking music. Soaking music is music without words, used to quiet your body and soul down.

Continue to speak to Jesus in your prayer language (tongues). Worship in tongues out loud to the Father until you feel a shift in atmosphere.

As you feel the presence of Jesus in the room increase, you may want to sit or lie down to get your body and soul even more quiet. Stay focused on Jesus and don't let your mind wander off.

While you are sitting or lying down in Jesus' presence, talk to Him. You can ask Jesus questions like, "Jesus what do think of me?" Then wait for his response.

Jesus may show you a picture of the two of you together holding hands walking on the beach or in a field of flowers.

At this intimate time, it is all about trusting Jesus.

Allow your spirit to engage with Jesus.

The Holy Spirit has brought you to Jesus. Now allow Jesus to enjoy your presence.

Highlights

- Make the time

- Turn on praise or soaking music

- Sing in tongues out loud

- Read scriptures out loud

- Transition to soaking or worship music

- Pray in tongues until you feel the shift in the atmosphere

- Sit or lay down

- Talk to Jesus

- Stay focused on Jesus and the Father

- Listen, look, feel

- Trust

But what IF you can't hear or see HIM?

At this point, if you are having a tough time hearing or seeing Jesus, then ask Him, "Jesus is there anyone I need to forgive?"

Sometimes unforgiveness, unbelief, fear, or lies block us from hearing or seeing Jesus.

After Jesus tells you who to forgive and you forgive them, give the bitterness and hurt to Jesus.

Then ask Jesus, "What do you give me in exchange?" It's going to be good, so receive in your heart what He gives you.

You may also continue asking Jesus questions like,

Is there anyone else I need to forgive?

Jesus, what do you think of me?

Jesus, show me a picture of us together.

Then trust what you see and hear.

This will unblock or open up your heart to receive more revelation from Jesus and the Father.

It is that easy!

But what does the bible say about encountering Jesus, and the Father?

Let's look at that next:

SESSION TWO: WHAT THE BIBLE SAYS

But a time is coming and is already here when the true worshipers will worship the Father in spirit and in truth; for the Father seeks such people to be His worshipers. God is spirit, and those who worship Him must worship in spirit and truth." (John 4:23-24)

- Your Father is seeking you to worship Him so He is not going to make it hard for you to spend time with Him.

- What does "in spirit" mean? You are a body, soul, and spirit – which we will cover later in Session Four.

- Worshipping the Father "in spirit" is more than singing songs in English or reading scriptures. Those are "in truth" so they engage your soul (your mind, will and emotions). The Father wants more than 'in truth' – He also wants, 'in spirit'.

- Worshipping in spirit engages your spirit with the Holy Spirit.

- Praying in tongues, using your prayer language, is another way to engage your spirit.

- You worship 'in spirit' with your spirit engaged. And 'in truth' you worship with your mind, reason, and logic engaged.

- What does 'in truth' mean? It means to be yourself. He knows you and loves you just the way you are. Reading scriptures are the truth, so you can read His word back to Him, the Father.

> **Therefore, believers, since we have confidence and full freedom to enter the Holy Place [the place where God dwells] by the blood of Jesus, by this new and living way which He initiated and opened for us through the veil [as in the Holy of Holies], that is, through His flesh. And since we have a great and wonderful Priest [Who rules] over the house of God, let us approach [God] with a true and sincere heart in unqualified assurance of faith, having had our hearts sprinkled clean from an evil conscience and our bodies washed with pure water. (Hebrews 10:19-22)**

- Reread that verse and add your name each time you see, 'believers' 'we' 'us' or 'our'.

- This verse is speaking to you as a believer if you have accepted Jesus as Lord of your life.

- Jesus' blood qualifies you and gives you full freedom and confidence to enter the place where God dwells.

- Asking Jesus to forgive you of your sins, washes and purifies you, which makes your heart sprinkled clean of an evil conscience. It is all about Jesus making you clean by His death and resurrection.

- I know it seems like we should have to do more cleansing, more washing, more groveling. Especially when we have a lot to be forgiven for. But Jesus' blood is enough! What Jesus did on the cross is enough to wash and cleanse us of all of our sins.

- It is not about quoting scriptures over and over, or telling Jesus how you messed up. That is nauseating and exhausting to Him when Jesus has already purified you by His blood.

- Jesus initiated and opened a way for you to step through the veil and to be with Him and the Father.

- Stepping through the veil is the same as saying 'stepping from the natural into the spiritual realm'.

- Stepping through the veil is as easy as stepping into your shower through the shower curtain.

- It is as easy as stepping through an opening onto a stage from the back of a stage. If you were ever in or watched a play or program being performed on a stage, you saw that when the time came the person would simply step through the curtain onto the stage. They didn't wrestle with the curtain – pulling, tugging, violently making their way through – that would be comical and weird. No they would simply just step over onto the stage.

- When you go from the kitchen into the living room you simply cross over from one room to the next, from one location to the next. Stepping into the spirit realm to be with Jesus is just that easy.

- Remember, it is not by your works or goodness or even groveling! Jesus made the way through the veil by opening it.

I am the Door; anyone who enters through Me will be saved, and will go in and out [freely], and find pasture (spiritual security). (John 10:9)

- Some people will physically practice stepping through a curtain or doorway over and over again to get it in their minds how easy it is when the Holy Spirit begins to draw them.

- When Jesus died, the veil in the temple was torn (Matthew 27:51), symbolizing that the way to the Father is now open for us to step through. The way is open for us to talk to the Father, and be with Him. Before Jesus came, only the high priest was allowed to enter into God's presence; and that, after much ceremonial cleansing.

- You have been adopted as His child. (Ephesians 1:5)

- Jesus wants a friend. Daddy God wants HIS Children To come HOME!

SESSION THREE: HOLY SPIRIT AND YOUR SPIRIT

**He came and preached peace to you who were far away
and peace to those who were near. For through Him
(Jesus) we both have access to the Father by one Spirit.
(Holy Spirit) (Ephesians 2:17-18)**

- We have access to the Father by the Holy Spirit because of what Jesus has done.

**And I will ask the Father, and He will give you another
Helper (Comforter, Advocate, Intercessor, Counselor,
Strengthener, Standby), to be with you forever – the
Spirit of Truth, whom the world cannot receive [and take
to its heart] because it does not see Him or know Him,
but you know Him because He (the Holy Spirit) remains
with you continually and will be in you. (John 14:16-17)**

- The Holy Spirit is your guide.

- The Holy Spirit speaks to your spirit. He will lead you to Jesus, and Jesus leads you to the Father.

- You don't want to go to the Father without Jesus or the Holy Spirit leading.

- With Jesus and the Holy Spirit we have access to the Father. We have full freedom and confidence to enter into God's holy place by His Holy Spirit.

- Who knows you more than your spirit? No-one! Who knows God more than His Spirit? No-one!

Practice to Develop Your Spirit Man

**But solid food is for the [spiritually] mature, whose
senses are trained by practice to distinguish between
what is morally good and what is evil. (Hebrews 5:14)**

- You can't be more spiritual any more than you can be more human. You are already a spiritual being so you can't be more spiritual. But you can exercise your spiritual senses by practice.

- You must practice developing your spiritual senses to make them stronger, sensitive and energized with power.

- Practice discerning. When you meet people what do you discern? Or when you walk into a room what do you discern?

**I pray that out of His glorious riches He may strengthen
you with power through His Spirit in your inner self,
[indwelling your innermost being and personality].
(Ephesians 3:16)**

- You can develop your spirit and inner man through praying in tongues.

- The Holy Spirit is your guide and brings revelation from the Father to your spirit.

**But just as it is written [in Scripture], "Things which
the eye has not seen and the ear has not heard, and
which have not entered the heart of man, all that
GOD has prepared for those who love [who hold
Him in affectionate reverence, who obey Him, and**

who gratefully recognize the benefits that He has bestowed]." For God has unveiled them and revealed them to us through the [Holy] Spirit; for the Spirit searches all things [diligently], even [sounding and measuring] the [profound] depths of God [the divine counsels and things far beyond human understanding]. (1 Corinthians 2:9-10)

Tongues

- Praying in tongues builds up your faith. (Jude 1:20)

- Praying in tongues is praying the Holy Spirit's language or words. It engages and strengthens your spirit man.

- Praying in tongues and then quoting scriptures is engaging your spirit and soul – which builds up your heart, mind, and emotions. Doing this causes depression or discouragement to leave and brings encouragement and strength.

- Meditating on the word helps strengthen your inner man too. As the word gets in your heart, your spirit opens up because your spirit trusts the word of God. Your spirit and your soul together will begin to believe what the word says.

He will be like a tree planted by streams of water, which yields its fruit in season and whose leaf does not wither. Whatever he does prospers. (Psalms 1:3)

- As the word gets into your heart, your spirit opens up and is strengthened. God's life will flow into your body, soul and spirit.

One with the Holy Spirit

But the one who is united and joined to the Lord is ONE spirit with Him. (1 Corinthians 6:17)

- Declare this scripture out loud like you mean it! "I am one, united to the Lord, and I am joined to the Lord, I am one spirit with Him!"

- You have full access to the realm of God all the time because you are one spirit with Him. You are united and joined to the Lord.

- The Holy Spirit is one with God and is now in you. Where you go, He goes all the time; you have full access to the presence of God all the time.

- When you were born again and made Jesus the LORD of your life, Jesus came into you with the Holy Spirit and you were made as one with Them.

- The Holy Spirit gives your spirit ideas, thoughts, words, pictures. He also energizes your body.

And if the Spirit of Him who raised Jesus from the dead lives in you, He who raised Christ Jesus from the dead will also give life to your mortal bodies through His Spirit, who lives in you. (Romans 8:11)

The Holy Spirit speaks mainly in 3 ways

- PICTURES:

  The Holy Spirit may give you a picture in your mind or your sanctified imagination. As you trust the Holy Spirit and stay focused on the picture that He is showing you, He will elaborate or expound the picture. He may begin to turn the picture into a movie or events that have, or are now, or will take place.

- WORDS:

  You will hear in your spirit, words. Hearing words may start off sounding like your voice. But after practice, you will be able to distinguish between the Father, Jesus and the Holy Spirit's voice. The Father, Jesus and the Holy Spirit each have their own voice and individually they all want to speak to you.

- FEELINGS:

  You will begin to feel: joy, peace, love, rest, acceptance, hope, oneness, fulfillment, life, forgiveness, unity and so much more that you have not yet experienced in its fullness while on earth.

- Say right now, "Holy Spirit I receive everything you have for me."

Praise and Worship

- Praise and worship will strengthen your inner man

- The joy of the Lord is your strength. (Nehemiah 8:10b)

- Learning to rejoice in the Lord is using your soul (which is your mind, will, emotions) and using your body.

- Paul says, "Rejoice in the Lord … and the peace of God will guard your heart and minds. (Philippians 4:4,7)

- If you would sing out loud, clap, quote scriptures out loud on purpose with energy not just mouthing and going through the motions, your strength would return and you would be energized, and full of peace and joy.

- Laughter and joy strengthens your spirit and soul. Watch funny movies, and enjoy life. This frees up your spirit and keeps your heart soft.

- Keep your heart as tender as the heart of a child's.

"I assure you and most solemnly say to you, unless you repent [that is, change your inner self—your old way of thinking to live changed lives, and become like children (trusting, humble, and forgiving)], you will never enter the kingdom of heaven. (Matthew 18:3)

SESSION FOUR: BODY / SOUL / SPIRIT

Body

God has designed you with a body, soul, and spirit.

- You have a physical body that has five senses: You see, hear, smell, taste, and touch, so you can interact with the physical world.

- You have a soul: It's your mind, will, and emotions, your memories, experiences and filters or walls that you may have built to protect yourself.

- Your body and soul make up your flesh man. We will cover more about your soul later in this session.

- You can declare scriptures over your body to cause them to come into alignment with the word of God.

> **And if the Spirit (Holy Spirit) of Him (God) who raised Jesus from the dead lives in you, He (Holy Spirit) who raised Christ Jesus from the dead will also give life to your mortal bodies through His Spirit, who lives in you. (Romans 8:11)**

- Remember Jesus had been dead for three days. His flesh was in bad shape but yet the Holy Spirit came and brought enough life to Jesus' body that it became alive.

- Every organ, all cells, blood vessels, and the skin covering were restored and energized with life.

- Jesus' body came into alignment with the word of God.

Soul

- The soul is the Mind, Will, Emotions, Memories, Experiences, and Walls

- Concerning memories – good or bad – the Holy Spirit will give you a word, a thought, or an impression. And then, your previous experience will determine if your soul receives from Him or not!

- For example, the Holy Spirit may speak to your spirit and give you a word about a lady you see in Walmart. But the lady reminds you of your mother. Now, depending on your relationship with your mother, your soul will decide if your body will go or not go to the lady at Walmart and give her the word from the Holy Spirit.

My sheep hear My voice and I know them and they follow Me. (John 10:27)

- The scripture above says you hear Him, so declare this to your soul and spirit, "I hear the voice of the Lord. Soul, you will come into alignment, spirit you will come into alignment with the voice of the Holy Spirit".

- Your brain/soul/heart will fight you, so you have to stay out of your head.

- Also, when you speak down to yourself or allow your soul to think badly of yourself, it hurts Jesus. He is so in love with you, therefore when you degrade or think less of yourself than he does of you, it hurts him. Jesus thinks of you as his overcoming bride, pure without spot or blemish, mighty warrior, best friend, his joy the one He died for. You are the one He went to the cross for, so do not degrade yourself!

- You must speak hope to your soul when your soul/heart feels downcast, disturbed, restless, or disquieted. Read in Psalms where David is speaking to his soul:

But let all who take refuge in you be glad, let them ever sing for joy. (Psalms 5:11)

He restores my soul. (Psalms 23:3)

Why are you downcast O, my soul? Why so disturbed within me? Put your hope in God for I will yet praise Him, my Savior, and my God. (Psalms 42:5)

Why are you downcast, (despair, restless, disquieted) Oh my soul? Put your hope in God, for I will yet praise Him, my Savior, and my God. (Psalms 42:11)

- Remember you are in Jesus. This is the place you must step back into if you step out. This is the place where you live and pray. This is the place where you will find peace and joy.

So that He might sanctify the church, having cleansed her by the washing of water with the word [of God], so that [in turn] He might present the church to Himself in glorious splendor, without spot or wrinkle or any such thing; but that she would be holy [set apart for God] and blameless. (Ephesians 5:26-27)

Once you were alienated from God and were enemies in your minds because of your evil behavior. But now He has reconciled you by Christ's physical body through death to present you holy in His sight without blemish and free from accusations. (Colossians1:21-22)

- Declare out loud what the word says, because your soul will respond to the word of God!

- You can also sing the word over your soul/heart. Praise Jesus out loud declaring, He is your Savior and God.

- Declare, "I put my hope in you Lord. Jesus, you have made me a spotless, pure, glorious bride, blameless in your sight. I am pure and I run to you without a heart that condemns me. You guide me in paths of righteousness. You anoint my head with oil, goodness, and love will follow me all the days of my life. I will dwell in your house forever."

- Soon you will begin to feel your soul/heart being restored with hope, peace, confidence, and love.

Giving thanks to the Father who has qualified (you) to share in the inheritance of the saints in the Kingdom of Light. (Colossians 1:12)

- He has qualified you to share in the Kingdom that is full of light!

Spirit

- You have a spirit:

  When you pass away your spirit man leaves the body. When your heart stops both your soul and spirit depart.

- Your soul and spirit make up your spirit man. Your soul and body make up your flesh man.

  Now it happened that the poor man died and his spirit was carried away by the angels to Abraham's bosom (paradise), and the rich man also died and was buried. In Hades (the realm of the dead), being in torment, he looked up and saw Abraham far away and Lazarus in his bosom (paradise). And he cried out, 'Father Abraham, have mercy on me, and send Lazarus so that he may dip the tip of his finger in water and cool my tongue, because I am in severe agony in this flame.' But Abraham said, 'Son, remember that in your lifetime you received your good things [all the comforts and delights], and Lazarus likewise bad things [all the discomforts and distresses]; but now he is comforted here [in paradise], while you are in severe agony. (Luke 16:22-25)

- This scripture says the poor man's spirit was carried away, and then it says the rich man looked up and saw, and could remembered. Your spirit has a mouth and can speak, so it has a voice. Your spirit has eyes, fingers, a tongue and gets thirsty. Your spirit can be tormented just as it can have peace.

- The rich man's soul remembered what life was like. Your soul remembers and understands. He asked for Lazarus to dip the tip of his finger in the water.

- In your soul/mind, you will remember your family on the earth.

- James 2:26 ... just as the human body without the spirit is dead... .

- In death, your body stays on the earth but your spirit goes to heaven, if you are born again.

- Your spirit man has arms, hands, and fingers.

- Your spirit man has a head, hair, ears, eyes, nose, and mouth.

- Your spirit man has feet and toes, it looks just like you. That's one way you know each other in heaven.

Then Moses, Aaron, Nadab, and Abihu, and seventy of the elders of Israel went up [the mountainside], and they saw [a manifestation of] the God of Israel; and under His feet there appeared to be a pavement of sapphire, just as clear as the sky itself. Yet He did not stretch out His hand against the nobles of the Israelites, and they saw [the manifestation of the presence of] God, and ate and drank. (Exodus 24:9-11)

- In this scripture Moses and the elders "saw" so their spirit man had eyes to see with.

- They saw God's feet, so God has feet. He has a spirit "body". God is not a big vapor or wispy wind, neither are you.

- The verse says God stretched out His hand.

- Your spirit man has arms and hands just like God. It also says they ate and drank. Your spirit man has a mouth, teeth, and can eat and drink.

- Just like your body has senses, your spirit man has senses.

- When you sleep at night your body sleeps but your spirit is always awake.

- You can see in the spirit realm with your spiritual eyes. You can see the angels with your spiritual eyes (unless the angels appear in the natural). You will see Jesus with your spiritual eyes (unless He appears to you in the natural).

- You can hear Jesus' voice, the Holy Spirits' voice, and the Father's voice with your spiritual ears (unless they speak audibly, and then you'll hear them with your physical ears).

- You can smell the presence of Jesus with your spiritual nose. Some say He smells like flowers or perfume.

- You can feel His presence around you. You may feel peace, joy or love when you walk into a room.

- You can taste His presence with your spiritual mouth. Some have said that suddenly they tasted honey even though they were not eating.

SESSION FIVE: WHAT JESUS SAYS

I am the gate, whoever enters through ME will be saved.
He will come in and go out and find pasture. (John 10:9)

- In this scripture, I want you to see that it says you will 'come in and go out'. You can go in the spirit realm and come out, then go back in again. You can also be in both places at the same time.

- Jesus says, "I only do what I see MY Father doing."

- You are a spirit who sees in the spirit realm but at the same time can be in your fleshly body standing talking to someone.

In that hour Jesus rejoiced in the Spirit and said, "I
thank You, Father, Lord of heaven and earth, that You
have hidden these things from the wise and prudent
(religious) and revealed them to babes. (Luke 10:21)

- I once had a pastor say to me, "Why would God show you these things in heaven? I have been serving Him for 40 years. I have been pastoring for 20, and you are still wet behind the ears. And I thought to myself, "Well, I guess THAT'S why God is showing me these things in heaven!"

- Don't think you have to be old, or know everything in the bible. Stay tenderhearted and childlike trusting Him.

- Stay unoffendable.

- Watch the words you speak, and beware of the things you see and listen to as well.

- Keep a pure heart.

He replied, "... because the knowledge of the secrets
of the KINGDOM OF HEAVEN (or the place where
GOD dwells) has been given to you, but not to them.
Whoever has will be given more, and they will have an
abundance... . (Matthew 13:11-12)

- Declare this out loud. Say, "The secrets of the KINGDOM OF HEAVEN
  have been given to ME and even more will be given to me, in abundance."

And He said to them, "To you it has been given to know
the mystery of the kingdom of God; (The kingdom of
GOD is the place where GOD dwells, it is where HIS
throne is located.) (Mark 4:11)

- Declare this out loud. Say, "I know the mystery of the Kingdom of God. It
  has been given to me to know, therefore I know and receive".

And [that you may come] to know [practically, through
personal experience] the love of Christ which far
surpasses [mere] knowledge [without experience], that
you may be filled up [throughout your being] to all
the fullness of God [so that you may have the richest
experience of God's presence in your lives, completely
filled and flooded with God Himself]. (Ephesian 3:19)

- Jesus wants you (through personal experience, not from hearing someone
  else's experience) to feel and experience the fullness of His love. Once you
  have experienced His love for yourself, no-one can take it away.

- Nothing and no one can satisfy you like Jesus' love for you.

- He wants you to feel and experience Him, and be filled up with the fullness of GOD.

- God wants you to experience Him. God wants you filled and flooded with Himself, so HE made a way for you to be that. God made it easy and simple for us to experience Him.

We are Made One

The Father is in Me and I am in the Father. (John 10:38)

- Declare this out loud, "The Father is in Me and I am in the Father, we are ONE!"

On that day [when that time comes] you will know for yourselves that I (Jesus) am in My Father, and you are in Me, and I am in you. (John 14:20)

- Declare this out loud, "Jesus is in the Father, I am in Jesus, Jesus is in me, therefore I am in the Father also."

- The Father is in Heaven seated in His Kingdom. We are seated in the Father in the Kingdom of Heaven.

- Ask for a revelation of this. I don't want you to just have a head knowledge of this, but revelation. Where the Father goes, we can go too. What the Father sees, we can see too.

How to Access Jesus in the Heavenly Realm

**Nothing in all of creation is hidden from God's sight.
(Hebrews 4:13)**

- We are in the Father because of Jesus. When the scripture reads, "in all of creation," that means everything that was ever created. He sees the stars, planets, angels, the throne room, and what is going on in the throne room: it is all in plain sight of the Father. The people that have passed away are also in plain view of the Father and Jesus.

- We are in Him, and with our spirit eyes, not our natural eyes, we also have access to see, hear, taste and feel that realm.

- Jesus saw the rich man and Lazarus in Abraham's bosom. Jesus didn't see and hear the conversation with His natural ears. These people were not hidden from God's sight just because they were not on the earth any longer.

**Nothing, (this means NOTHING), in all of creation is
hidden from God's sight. (Luke 16:24)**

SESSION SIX: LOVE THE LORD WITH ALL YOUR HEART

**Love the Lord your GOD with all your heart, all your
soul, and all your mind. (Matthew 22:37)**

- But what if you don't? (I'm glad you asked!) What if you have issues with trust or fear?

- Once you realize you DO have issues with fear or trust, this would be a good time to stop.

- Let's stop and ask the Father. Say, "Father, is their someone I need to forgive?"

- The first face or name that comes to mind is a clue. So say, "I choose to forgive _____ for _____ ."

- Say, "Father, I hand to you all the bitterness and hurt that this person(s), has caused me to feel."

- Then say, "Father, what good thing do you give me in exchange?"

- You may ask the Father, "Are there any lies I have believed about you?"

- If He says, "Yes," then ask the Father what it is and who taught you this lie. Then forgive them. Ask the Father, "What good thing do you give me in exchange?"

- Continue to do this until the Holy Spirit stops bringing people to mind, until your heart feels light and free.

**Trust in the Lord with all your heart and lean not on
your own understanding. (Psalms 3:5)**

- I was able to see Jesus in heaven even though I had a lot of issues with trust, hurt, and fears. So, don't let the devil tell you, you have too many issues.

- Once you begin stepping over into heaven through the veil and spending time with Jesus, He will heal your heart and will reveal things you didn't even know. Jesus wants you with Him. He has made a way for you to be with Him just the way you are. His blood cleanses and purifies us.

- Declare Psalms 32:8 over your heart and soul. "I will guide you along the best path for your life. I will advise you and watch over you." Reread that verse and insert your name every place it says, "you" or "your".

- Declare: "Because of God's promises, I will not fear. I loose all fear, I loose all bitterness, I loose all jealousy, unforgiveness, condemnation, and all accusations from my heart and soul. I receive the blood of Jesus to cleanse and purify me now! I am made whole now!"

- Then pray in your prayer language (pray in tongues) for a moment and receive any direction from the Holy Spirit that he may bring to mind.

TESTIMONIES about Kim Robinson's book, "Heaven is real and FUN!"

- *I read this book when it first came out and thought it was great. I listen to Kat Kerr so a lot of the information in this book was confirmed by her. Heaven IS FUN and most Christians do not know it. They need to lighten up and believe the best about the Father. Robin Bremer*

- *Looking forward to the children's book! I can't begin to tell you how many things God has shown me/told me since reading your book. I haven't actually taken a trip to heaven yet, but I feel closer to Him and have told many people about you and your YouTube videos. P.M.*

- *Your book brought hope back to bringing me closer to our Father and Jesus. Thank you for that. I can't wait til your fun kid's book comes out so I can share it with my daughter. Thanks so much for recommending John Tussey Healing Sounds and your video How to hear God's voice and step over into His presence. M.*

- *I have read many Christian books on people visiting Heaven and I must say this is now one of my favorites! If you like the Author Kat Kerr you will love this book by Kim Robinson. It is a well written account of what awaits us in Heaven!!! R.B.*

- *Enjoyed every page of this book. I highly recommend it to anyone searching for the love of God in their life! C.*

- *An amazing book, that will have you longing for heaven. Very simply written but with so much depth of what God's love is really about. L.*

- *This book made me laugh, cry, shout with joy and most of all brought me to a deeper understanding of our Father God, Jesus Christ, and the Holy Spirit. Your relationship with them is so precious and this book will help you see they're not so serious all the time! Get ready for your soul to be delighted by the glory and love of God Amen! H.*

- *It's an awesome book. K.B.*

- *Great book. I wrote the author and she actually responded. N.L.*

- *Love this book! L.F.*

- *Great. Author is just as nice in person. A.H.*

- *Kim reads her book better than a professional could. Take advantage of the faith, emotion and conviction she puts into the text. You're not just after knowledge, here. Position yourself for the impact this can have on your spirit man. I listen to it repeatedly allowing it to create a grid inside of me. C.M.*

- *I thought it was amazing and couldn't put it down! A.C.*

- *This book gave me an unquenchable desire to be with my Lord Jesus! And I'm going to keep reading Kim's book because every time I do, it takes me to Heaven – currently in my imagination – but I'm sure one day I'll have a real visit! D.L.*

Printed in Great Britain
by Amazon

20107740R10027